My First Airplane Trip

Solve Problems Involving Measurement

Amelia Erickson

INFOMAX
MATH READERS

Rosen
Classroom™

New York

Published in 2015 by The Rosen Publishing Group, Inc.
29 East 21st Street, New York, NY 10010

Book Design: Katelyn Londino

Photo Credits: Cover ssuaphotos/Shutterstock.com; pp. 3–24 (background) LeksusTuss/Shutterstock.com; p. 5 travellight/
Shutterstock.com; p. 7 (living room) Blinka/Shutterstock.com; p. 7 (silver clock) Sergey Melnikov/Shutterstock.com;
p. 7 (wrist watch) ra2studio/Thinkstock.com; pp. 9, 11, 13, 15, 17,19, 21 (clock) rangizzz/Shutterstock.com; p. 11 Artazum
and Iriana Shiyan/Shutterstock.com; p. 13 Africa Studio/Shutterstock.com; p. 15 ileela/Shutterstock.com; pp. 17, 19 Digital
Vision/Thinkstock.com; p. 21 Rainer Lesniewski/Shutterstock.com; p. 22 bibiphoto/Shutterstock.com.

ISBN: 978-1-4777-4606-6
6-pack ISBN: 978-1-4777-4608-0

Manufactured in the United States of America

CPSIA Compliance Information: Batch #WS15RC: For further information contact Rosen Publishing, New York, New York at 1-800-237-9932.

Contents

Going to California   4

How to Tell Time   8

Travel Day Is Here   10

At the Airport   14

Time for Takeoff   18

Time to Land   22

Glossary   23

Index   24

Going to California

I like to travel. I've taken long car trips to other states. I've been on boats and trains. But I've never been on a plane. It won't be that way for long, though. My family and I are going on a trip to California.

California is far away from where I live. That's why we're taking a plane to get there. I'm excited for my first airplane trip. My dad says the ground looks very small when you're up in the air. I can't wait to see what it looks like.

Planes fly very high in the air. They go higher than the clouds! →

My family is leaving for California tomorrow. We know our flight leaves at a certain time. We have to give ourselves enough time to get up, get ready, and get to the airport on time. If we don't stay on time, the plane might leave without us!

The best way to stay on time is to always know what time it is. I learned how to tell time in school, so I can help my parents stay on **schedule**. When they ask me what time it is, I know I can tell them.

I know how to tell time on clocks and watches. Their faces look the same. →

How to Tell Time

Telling time is easy when you know how to read a clock. Some clocks are labeled with the numbers 1 through 12. They **represent** hours. A short hand on the clock points to these numbers. It's called the hour hand.

Clocks also have 60 hash marks that represent minutes, and 60 minutes equal 1 hour. They're separated into groups of 5. A longer hand, called the minute hand, points to the minute. When I read and write time, I always record the hour first, then the minutes.

Sometimes I think of a clock as a curled number line that stretches from 0 to 60. I know the minutes reset to 0 when I reach the 60-minute mark on a clock or number line.

Travel Day Is Here

California is far away from where I live, so it's going to take a long time to travel there by plane. I have to wake up early on the day of our flight.

I look at the clock on my wall when I wake up. The hour hand is pointing right at the 7. That means the hour is 7. The minute hand is pointing straight up to the top of the clock, which means there are 0 minutes. The hour hand and minute hand say it's 7:00 a.m.

The 60 hash marks on this number line represent all the minutes that are in the 7 o'clock hour. Since there are 0 minutes in 7:00, I can't draw a line yet.

minutes

My dad says we have to leave our house no later than 7:45 a.m. That's 45 minutes from now. I have to do a few things to get ready before we go. First, I brush my teeth. That takes 5 minutes. Adding 5 minutes to 7:00 makes it 7:05 a.m.

Next, I pack my backpack with everything I want to use on the plane. I pack a book and some homework. It takes me 20 minutes. What time is it now?

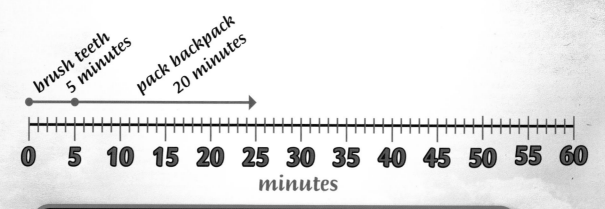

I can skip count by 5s to help me tell time. I count 1 group of 5 minutes to reach 7:05, the time I finish brushing my teeth. I count 4 groups of 5 minutes, or 20 minutes, to reach 7:25. That's when I finish packing my backpack.

get up

brush teeth

pack backpack

13

At the Airport

Soon, we leave our house, and we're on our way to the airport. We check in for our flight and go through a security gate. Then, we make our way to the gate where our plane is waiting.

When we get to our gate, my mom asks me what time it is. I look at my watch. The hour hand is in between the 9 and the 10. Since the hand hasn't reached the 10 yet, I know the hour is 9 o'clock. Where is the minute hand pointing?

Minutes are shown in groups of 5, so I can count by 5s until I reach the minute hand. I count 6 groups of 5. There are a few minutes left over, so now I'll count by 1s. I count 33 minutes altogether. It's 9:33 a.m.

33 minutes

0 5 10 15 20 25 30 35 40 45 50 55 60

minutes

After a while, an airline worker announces the flight is **boarding**. That means we can finally get on the plane! I look at my watch. It's 10:11 a.m.

Boarding goes pretty fast. My parents and I find our seats in the middle of the plane. We put our bags away, sit down, and **fasten** our seat belts. When I look at my watch next, 26 minutes have passed. What time is it now? Add 26 minutes to 10:11 a.m. to find out.

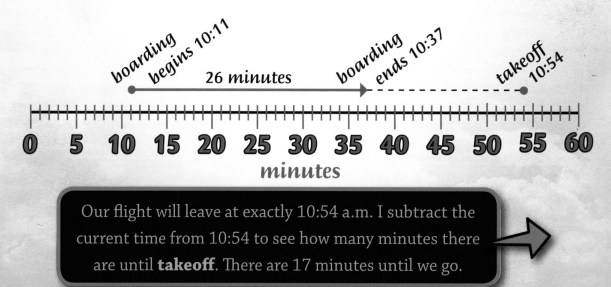

Our flight will leave at exactly 10:54 a.m. I subtract the current time from 10:54 to see how many minutes there are until **takeoff**. There are 17 minutes until we go.

10:11 + 0:26 = 10:37

10:54 − 10:37 = 0:17

boarding time

boarding ends

takeoff

Time for Takeoff

After 17 minutes of waiting, the pilot announces that we're ready for takeoff. The plane's engines get very loud, and the plane starts moving very fast. Once the wheels leave the **runway**, we're in the air! Everything on the ground gets smaller as the plane gets higher.

I look out the window for a while. After that, I decide to read my book. I start reading at 12:19 p.m. I stop at 12:54 p.m. How many minutes did I spend reading?

I can count back on the clock by 1s and 5s. I move 4 minutes back, then back by 6 groups of 5, then back by 1 more minute. Together, that makes 35 minutes.

18

12:54 − 12:19 = 0:35

started reading

finished reading

35 minutes

minutes

19

The flight to California is very long. I start to get sleepy. I fall asleep for a few hours. When I wake up, it's almost time to land!

California is so far away that the **time zone** changes. The time there is 3 hours earlier than where I live. When we land, it says it's 4:14 p.m. on my watch. But it's actually 1:14 p.m. in California, since it's 3 hours earlier. I can set my watch so it matches California time. What's different about the clocks on the next page? What about them is the same?

The only difference between these clocks is the hour. The minute hand doesn't change when you change time zones. →

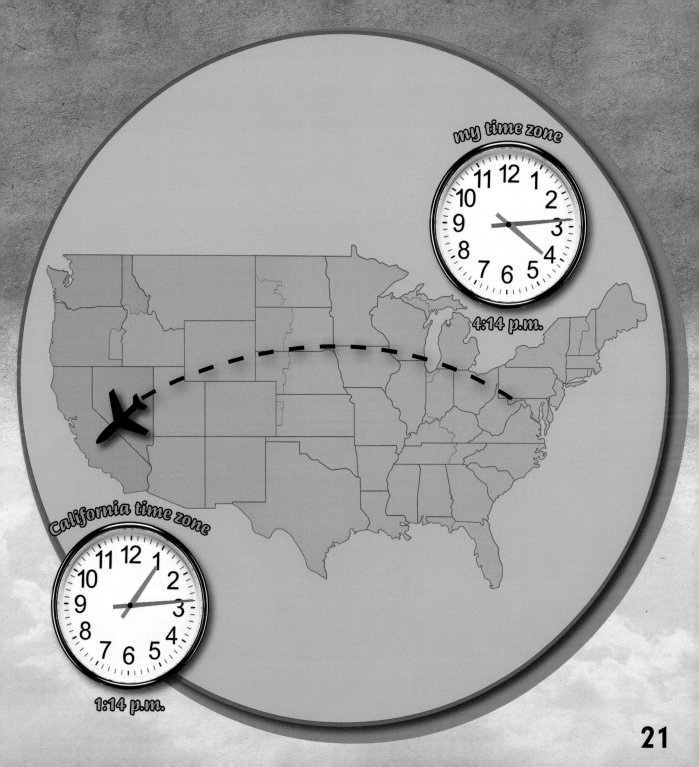

my time zone

4:14 p.m.

California time zone

1:14 p.m.

Time to Land

At the end of the flight, the pilot announces that he's going to land the plane. As the pilot lands the plane, I can feel us going lower and lower. It feels weird!

The pilot does a good job landing the plane. He slows the plane down and makes sure we get to the airport gate safely. Now that we've landed, my first airplane trip is over. I can't wait for my next plane trip—the flight back home!

Glossary

board (BOHRD) To get on a plane, train, or boat.

fasten (FAA-suhn) To make secure.

represent (reh-prih-ZEHNT) To stand for.

runway (RUHN-way) A strip of smooth ground along which an aircraft takes off and lands.

schedule (SKEH-jool) A plan for what to do and when to do it.

takeoff (TAY-koff) The action of rising from the ground into the air.

time zone (TYME zohn) An area of land where a common standard time is used.

Index

airport, 6, 14, 22

flight, 6, 10, 14, 16, 20, 22

gate, 14, 22

hash marks, 8, 10

hour hand, 8, 9, 10, 14

hours, 8, 10, 14, 20

land, 20, 22

minute hand, 8, 9, 10, 14, 20

minutes, 8, 9, 10, 11, 12, 14,
        15, 16, 18, 19

number line, 8, 10

plane, 4, 6, 10, 12, 14, 16, 18,
        22

schedule, 6

skip count, 12

takeoff, 16, 17, 18

time zone, 20, 21

trip, 4, 22